KT-406-207

*To*

_____

*From*

_____

*Date*

_____

*Message*

_____

_____

# My
# LITTLE
# BOOK OF
## *promises*

christian
art gifts

*My Little Book of Promises*

© 2002 Christian Art Gifts, RSA
Christian Art Gifts Inc., IL, USA

Compiled by Wilma Le Roux
Designed by Christian Art Gifts

Christian Art Gifts has made every effort to trace the ownership of all quotes and poems in this book. In the event of any question that may arise from the use of any quote or poem, we regret any error made and will be pleased to make the necessary correction in future editions of this book.

Unless otherwise indicated, Scripture taken from the *Holy Bible*, New International Version®. NIV®. Copyright © 1973, 1978, 1984 by International Bible Society. Used by permission of Zondervan Publishing House. All rights reserved.

ISBN 1-86920-062-4

Printed in China

03  04  05  06  07  08  09  10  11  12  –  11  10  9  8  7  6  5  4  3  2

# Contents

Everyone should be quick to listen, slow to speak and slow to become angry, for man's anger does not bring about the righteous life that God desires.

*James 1:19-20*

In your anger do not sin: Do not let the sun go down while you are still angry, and do not give the devil a foothold.

*Ephesians 4:26-27*

Now you must rid yourselves of all such things as these: anger, rage, malice, slander and filthy language from your lips.

*Colossians 3:8*

*A joyful heart is the inevitable result of a heart burning with love.*

*Mother Teresa*

# Anger

In your anger do not sin; when you are on your beds, search your hearts and be silent. Offer right sacrifices and trust in the Lord.

*Psalm 4:4-5*

Refrain from anger and turn from wrath; do not fret – it leads only to evil.

*Psalm 37:8*

Do not be quickly provoked in your spirit, for anger resides in the lap of fools.

*Ecclesiastes 7:9*

*Forgiveness is the fragrance the violet sheds on the heel that has crushed it.*

*Mark Twain*

"You have heard that it was said to the people long ago, 'Do not murder, and anyone who murders will be subject to judgment.' But I tell you that anyone who is angry with his brother will be subject to judgment."

*Matthew 5:21-22*

A gentle answer turns away wrath, but a harsh word stirs up anger.

*Proverbs 15:1*

Get rid of all bitterness, rage and anger, brawling and slander, along with every form of malice. Be kind and compassionate to one another, forgiving each other, just as in Christ God forgave you.

*Ephesians 4:31-32*

*You are what you think about all day long.*
*Robert Schuller*

# Death

Christ has indeed been raised from the dead, the firstfruit of those who have fallen asleep. For since death came through a man, the resurrection of the dead comes also through a man.

*1 Corinthians 15:20-21*

Even though I walk through the valley of the shadow of death, I will fear no evil, for You are with me; Your rod and Your staff, they comfort me.

*Psalm 23:4*

God will redeem my life from the grave; He will surely take me to Himself.

*Psalm 49:15*

*Death cannot harm me because it is a stingless bee; its stinger is lodged in Christ.*

*Peter J. Kreeft*

Where, O death, is your victory?
Where, O death, is your sting?

*1 Corinthians 15:55*

He will swallow up death forever. The Sovereign Lord will wipe away the tears from all faces; He will remove the disgrace of His people from all the earth.

*Isaiah 25:8*

"I tell you the truth, if anyone keeps My word, he will never see death."

*John 8:51*

*I am not tired of my work; neither am I tired of the world. Yet when Christ calls me Home, I shall go with the gladness of a schoolboy bounding away from school!*

*Adoniram Judson*

11

# Death

This grace ... has now been revealed through the appearing of our Savior, Christ Jesus, who has destroyed death and has brought life and immortality to light through the gospel.

*2 Timothy 1:9-10*

I have set the Lord always before me. Because He is at my right hand, I will not be shaken ... because You will not abandon me to the grave.

*Psalm 16:8, 10*

When calamity comes, the wicked are brought down, but even in death the righteous have a refuge.

*Proverbs 14:32*

*If a person has not found something to die for, that person isn't fit to live!*

*Dr. Martin Luther King, Jr.*

"But I tell you who hear Me: Love your enemies, do good to those who hate you, bless those who curse you, pray for those who mistreat you."

*Luke 6:27-28*

Do not take revenge, my friends, but leave room for God's wrath, for it is written: "It is Mine to avenge; I will repay," says the Lord.

*Romans 12:19*

If your enemy is hungry, give him food to eat; if he is thirsty, give him water to drink. In doing this, you will heap burning coals on his head ...

*Proverbs 25:21-22*

*The worst sin toward our fellow creatures is not to hate them, but to be indifferent to them.*

*George Bernard Shaw*

# Enemies

"Love your enemies, do good to them, and lend to them without expecting to get anything back. Then your reward will be great, and you will be sons of the Most High."

*Luke 6:35*

The Lord is with me; I will not be afraid. What can man do to me? The Lord is with me; He is my helper. I will look in triumph on my enemies.

*Psalm 118:6-7*

Love your enemies and pray for those who persecute you, that you may be sons of your Father.

*Matthew 5:44-45*

*If we could read the secret history of our enemies, we should find in each man sorrow and suffering enough to disarm all hostility.*

*Henry Wadsworth Longfellow*

# Eternal life

"I am the resurrection and the life. He who believes in Me will live, even though he dies; and whoever lives and believes in Me will never die."

*John 11:25-26*

... if you do these things, you will never fall, and you will receive a rich welcome into the eternal kingdom of our Lord and Savior Jesus Christ.

*2 Peter 1:10-11*

I write these things to you who believe in the name of the Son of God so that you may know that you have eternal life.

*1 John 5:13*

*We die daily. Happy are those who daily come to life as well.*

*George MacDonald*

# Eternal life

For our light and momentary troubles are achieving for us an eternal glory that far outweighs them all. So we fix our eyes not on what is seen, but on what is unseen. For what is seen is temporary, but what is unseen is eternal.

*2 Corinthians 4:17-18*

"My sheep listen to My voice; I know them, and they follow Me. I give them eternal life, and they shall never perish; no one can snatch them out of My hand."

*John 10:27-28*

"He who believes has everlasting life."

*John 6:47*

*It is in giving that we receive ... It is in dying that we are born to eternal life.*

*Francis of Assisi*

## Eternal life

This is the testimony: God has given us eternal life, and this life is in His Son.

*1 John 5:11*

"Whoever eats My flesh and drinks My blood has eternal life."

*John 6:54*

Now that you have been set free from sin ... the benefit you reap leads to holiness, and the result is eternal life. For the wages of sin is death, but the gift of God is eternal life in Christ Jesus our Lord.

*Romans 6:22-23*

*What is our light affliction when compared to such an eternity as this? Shame on us if we murmur and complain and turn back with such a heaven before our eyes!*

*J.C. Ryle*

# Failure

The Lord upholds all those who fall, and lifts up all who are bowed down.

*Psalm 145:14*

Thanks be to God, who always leads us in triumphal procession in Christ.

*2 Corinthians 2:14*

Though a righteous man falls seven times, he rises again, but the wicked are brought down by calamity.

*Proverbs 24:16*

*If you have made mistakes, even serious mistakes, there is always another chance for you. And supposing you have tried and failed again and again, you may have a fresh start any moment you choose, for this thing that we call "failure" is not the falling down, but the staying down.*

Mary Pickford

Faith is being sure of what we hope for and certain of what we do not see.

*Hebrews 11:1*

"I tell you the truth, anyone who has faith in Me will do what I have been doing. He will do even greater things than these, because I am going to the Father."

*John 14:12*

You are all sons of God through faith in Christ Jesus, for all of you who were baptized into Christ have clothed yourselves with Christ.

*Galatians 3:26-27*

*Faith is to believe what we do not see; and the reward of this faith is to see what we believe.*

*St. Augustine*

# Faith

I have been crucified with Christ and I no longer live, but Christ lives in me. The life I live in the body, I live by faith in the Son of God, who loved me and gave Himself for me.

*Galatians 2:20*

It is by grace you have been saved, through faith – and this not from yourselves, it is the gift of God – not by works, so that no one can boast.

*Ephesians 2:8-9*

The only thing that counts is faith expressing itself through love.

*Galatians 5:6*

*It is faith that brings power, not merely praying and weeping and struggling, but believing, daring to believe the written Word with or without feelings.*
*Catherine Booth*

Continue in what you have learned and have become convinced of, because you know those from whom you learned it, and how from infancy you have known the holy Scriptures, which are able to make you wise for salvation through faith in Christ Jesus.

*2 Timothy 3:14-15*

Be on your guard; stand firm in the faith; be men of courage; be strong.

*1 Corinthians 16:13*

The prayer offered in faith will make the sick person well; the Lord will raise him up.

*James 5:15*

*Faith is a resting of the heart in the sufficiency of the evidences.*

*Clark H. Pinnock*

## Faith

"Because you have seen me, you have believed; blessed are those who have not seen and yet have believed."

*John 20:29*

Without faith it is impossible to please God, because anyone who comes to Him, must believe that He exists and that He rewards those who earnestly seek Him.

*Hebrews 11:6*

We ... know that a man is not justified by observing the law, but by faith in Jesus Christ.

*Galatians 2:15-16*

*Faith rests on the naked word of God; that word believed gives full assurance.*

*H.A. Ironside*

These are written so that you may believe that Jesus is the Christ, the Son of God, and that by believing you may have life in His name.

*John 20:31*

"Have faith in God," Jesus answered. "I tell you the truth, if anyone says to this mountain, 'Go, throw yourself into the sea,' and does not doubt in his heart but believes that what he says will happen, it will be done for him."

*Mark 11:22-23*

"If you have faith as small as a mustard seed, you can say to this mulberry tree, 'Be uprooted and planted in the sea,' and it will obey you."

*Luke 17:6*

*Ten thousand difficulties do not make me doubt.*
*John Henry Newman*

# Faith

Faith comes from hearing the message, and the message is heard through the word of Christ.

*Romans 10:17*

We live by faith, not by sight.

*2 Corinthians 5:7*

This righteousness from God comes through faith in Jesus Christ to all who believe.

*Romans 3:22*

Fight the good fight of the faith. Take hold of the eternal life to which you were called.

*1 Timothy 6:12*

*Faith is the daring of the soul to go farther than it can see.*

*William N. Clarke*

I will refresh the weary and satisfy the faint.
*Jeremiah 31:25*

"Come to Me, all you who are weary and burdened, and I will give you rest. Take my yoke upon you and learn from Me, for I am gentle and humble in heart, and you will find rest for your souls."
*Matthew 11:28-29*

I will bind up the injured and strengthen the weak.
*Ezekiel 34:16*

"My grace is sufficient for you, for My power is made perfect in weakness."
*2 Corinthians 12:9*

*His strength is made perfect, not in our strength, but in our weakness.*

*Hannah Whitall Smith*

# Fatigue

He gives strength to the weary and increases the power of the weak. Even youths grow tired and weary, and young men stumble and fall; but those who hope in the Lord will renew their strength.

*Isaiah 40:29-30*

Cast your cares on the Lord and He will sustain you.

*Psalm 55:22*

*Life is a hard fight, a struggle, a wrestling with the principle of evil, hand to hand, foot to foot. Every inch of the way is disputed. The night is given us to take breath and to pray, to drink deep at the fountain of power. The day, to use the strength that has been given us, to go forth to work with it till the evening.*

*Florence Nightingale*

Be strong and courageous. Do not be terrified; do not be discouraged, for the Lord your God will be with you wherever you go.

*Joshua 1:9*

The Lord Himself goes before you and will be with you; He will never leave you nor forsake you. Do not be afraid; do not be discouraged.

*Deuteronomy 31:8*

Be strong and courageous. Do not be afraid or terrified ... for the Lord your God goes with you; He will never leave you nor forsake you.

*Deuteronomy 31:6*

*Give me one hundred preachers who fear nothing but sin and desire nothing but God ... such alone will shake the gates of hell and set up the kingdom of heaven on earth.*

*John Wesley*

27

# Fear

Do not let your hearts be troubled and do not be afraid.

*John 14:27*

Fear of a man will prove to be a snare, but whoever trusts in the Lord is kept safe.

*Proverbs 29:25*

So do not fear, for I am with you; do not be dismayed, for I am your God. I will strengthen you and help you; I will uphold you with My righteous right hand.

*Isaiah 41:10*

*Anxiety is the natural result when our hopes are centered in anything short of God and His will for us.*

*Billy Graham*

"Don't be afraid; just believe."

*Mark 5:36*

No harm will befall you, no disaster will come near your tent. For He will command His angels concerning you to guard you in all their ways.

*Psalm 91:10-11*

Then you will go on your way in safety, and your foot will not stumble; when you lie down, you will not be afraid; when you lie down, your sleep will be sweet. Have no fear of sudden disaster.

*Proverbs 3:23-25*

*Joy runs deeper than despair.*

*Corrie Ten Boom*

# Finances

Honor the Lord with your wealth, with the first-fruits of all your crops; then your barns will be filled to overflowing, and your vats will brim over with new wine.

*Proverbs 3:9-10*

"Bring the whole tithe into the storehouse, that there may be food in My house. Test Me in this," says the Lord Almighty, "and see if I will not throw open the floodgates of heaven and pour out so much blessing that you will not have room enough for it."

*Malachi 3:10*

*Just as our flesh is covered by clothing, and our blood is covered by our flesh, so are we, soul and body, covered and enclosed by the goodness of God.*
*Julian of Norwich*

Each man should give what he has decided in his heart to give, not reluctantly or under compulsion, for God loves a cheerful giver.

*2 Corinthians 9:7*

Whoever trusts in his riches will fall, but the righteous will thrive like a green leaf.

*Proverbs 11:28*

"Give, and it will be given to you. A good measure, pressed down, shaken together and running over, will be poured into your lap. For with the measure you use, it will be measured to you."

*Luke 6:38*

Godliness with contentment is great gain.

*1 Timothy 6:6*

*He who desires nothing but God is rich and happy.*
*Alphonsus Liguori*

# Forgiveness

Bear with each other and forgive whatever grievances you may have against one another. Forgive as the Lord forgave you.

*Colossians 3:13*

Repent, then, and turn to God, so that your sins may be wiped out, that times of refreshing may come from the Lord, and that He may send the Christ, who has been appointed for you – even Jesus.

*Acts 3:19-20*

If we confess our sins, He is faithful and just and will forgive us our sins and purify us from all unrighteousness.

*1 John 1:9*

*As by a Carpenter the world was made, only by that Carpenter can mankind be remade.*

*Desiderius Erasmus*

# Forgiveness

"If you forgive men when they sin against you, your heavenly Father will also forgive you. But if you do not forgive men their sins, your Father will not forgive your sins."

*Matthew 6:14-15*

Though your sins are like scarlet, they shall be as white as snow; though they are red as crimson, they shall be as wool.

*Isaiah 1:18*

"When you stand praying, if you hold anything against anyone, forgive him, so that your Father in heaven may forgive you your sins."

*Mark 11:25*

*I am to become a Christ to my neighbor and need to be for him what Christ is for me.*

*Martin Luther*

# Forgiveness

"Do not judge, and you will not be judged. Do not condemn, and you will not be condemned. Forgive, and you will be forgiven."

*Luke 6:37*

I said, "I will confess my transgressions to the Lord" – and You forgave the guilt of my sin.

*Psalm 32:5*

He forgave us all our sins, having canceled the written code, with its regulations, that was against us and that stood opposed to us; He took it away, nailing it to the cross.

*Colossians 2:13-14*

*The confession of evil works is the first beginning of good works.*

*Augustine of Hippo*

# Fruitfulness

If you remain in me and my words remain in you, ask whatever you wish, and it will be given you. This is to my Father's glory, that you bear much fruit.

*John 15:7-8*

That you may be able to discern what is best and may be pure and blameless until the day of Christ, filled with the fruit of righteousness that comes through Jesus Christ ...

*Philippians 1:10-11*

He is like a tree planted by streams of water, which yields its fruit in season and whose leaf does not wither. Whatever he does prospers.

*Psalm 1:3*

*Nothing can make a man truly great but being truly good, and partaking of God's holiness.*

*Matthew Arnold*

# Fruitfulness

But the fruit of the Spirit is love, joy, peace, patience, kindness, goodness, faithfulness, gentleness and self-control. Against such things there is no law.

*Galatians 5:22-23*

The righteous will flourish like a palm tree, they will grow like a cedar of Lebanon; planted in the house of the LORD, they will flourish in the courts of our God. They will still bear fruit in old age, they will stay fresh and green.

*Psalm 92:12-14*

*It is not what he has, or even what he does which expresses the worth of a man, but what he is.*

*Henri Amiel*

He saved us through the washing of rebirth and renewal by the Holy Spirit, whom He poured out on us generously through Jesus Christ our Savior, so that, having been justified by His grace, we might become heirs having the hope of eternal life.

*Titus 3:5-7*

In love He predestined us to be adopted as His sons through Jesus Christ, in accordance with His pleasure and will – to the praise of His glorious grace, which He has freely given us in the One He loves.

*Ephesians 1:4-6*

*You might say this is difficult for me to do – to know God. Yes it is. It is difficult for you to do. But it is not difficult for God to make himself known to you.*

*Brett Blair*

# Grace

All have sinned and fall short of the glory of God, and are justified freely by His grace through the redemption that came by Christ Jesus.

*Romans 3:23-24*

In Him we have redemption through His blood, the forgiveness of sins, in accordance with the riches of God's grace that He lavished on us with all wisdom and understanding.

*Ephesians 1:7-8*

*Our trials will seem to us nothing at all. We shall talk to one another about them in heaven ... Let us go on, therefore; and if the night be ever so dark, remember there is not a night that shall not have a morning ...*

*Charles Spurgeon*

God opposes the proud, but gives grace to the humble.

*James 4:6*

I always thank God for you because of His grace given you in Christ Jesus.

*1 Corinthians 1:4*

From the fullness of His grace we have all received one blessing after another.

*John 1:16*

Set your hope fully on the grace to be given you when Jesus Christ is revealed.

*1 Peter 1:13*

*A lot of Christians are going to get to heaven and find out that God offered so much more than they experienced.*

*Steve Brown*

# Grace

To each one of us grace has been given as Christ apportioned it.

*Ephesians 4:7*

Where sin increased, grace increased all the more, so that, just as sin reigned in death, so also grace might reign through righteousness to bring eternal life through Jesus Christ our Lord.

*Romans 5:20-21*

Now I commit you to God and to the word of His grace, which can build you up and give you an inheritance among all those who are sanctified.

*Acts 20:32*

*Grace is God Himself, His loving energy at work within His church and within our souls.*

*E. Underhill*

Sin shall not be your master, because you are not under law, but under grace.

*Romans 6:14*

God raised us up with Christ and seated us with Him in the heavenly realms in Christ Jesus, in order that in the coming ages He might show the incomparable riches of His grace.

*Ephesians 2:6-7*

God is able to make all grace abound to you, so that in all things at all times, having all that you need, you will abound in every good work.

*2 Corinthians 9:8*

*Heaven's rewards are all a matter of God's grace. They are God's generous recognition of selfless and sacrificial service.*

*J. Oswald Sanders*

## Grace

We have different gifts, according to the grace given us.

*Romans 12:6*

Grow in the grace and knowledge of our Lord and Savior Jesus Christ! To Him be the glory both now and forever!

*2 Peter 3:18*

If you return to the Lord, then your brothers and your children ... will come back to this land, for the Lord your God is gracious and compassionate. He will not turn His face from you if you return to Him.

*2 Chronicles 30:9*

*Four words destroyed slavery, "For whom Christ died."*

*T.R. Glover*

Let us then approach the throne of grace with confidence, so that we may receive mercy and find grace to help us in our time of need.

*Hebrews 4:16*

We have seen His glory, the glory of the One who came from the Father, full of grace and truth.

*John 1:14*

We believe it is through the grace of our Lord Jesus that we are saved ...

*Acts 15:11*

By the grace of God I am what I am, and His grace to me was not without effect.

*1 Corinthians 15:10*

*Grace is but glory begun, and glory is but grace perfected.*

*Jonathan Edwards*

# Grief

But You, O God, do see trouble and grief; You consider it to take it in hand.

*Psalm 10:14*

I will turn their mourning into gladness; I will give them comfort and joy instead of sorrow.

*Jeremiah 31:13*

I tell you the truth, you will weep and mourn while the earth rejoices. You will grieve, but your grief will turn to joy.

*John 16:20*

Godly sorrow brings repentance that leads to salvation and leaves no regret, but worldly sorrow brings death.

*2 Corinthians 7:10*

*Jesus knows all about sadness.*

*Alice Chapin*

God will wipe away every tear from their eyes.
*Revelation 7:17*

He will swallow up death forever. The Sovereign Lord will wipe away the tears from all faces ...
*Isaiah 25:8*

The Lord comforts His people and will have compassion on His afflicted ones.
*Isaiah 49:13*

The Lord is good to all; He has compassion on all He has made.
*Psalm 145:9*

*God weeps with us so that we may someday laugh with Him.*

*Jurgen Moltmann*

# Grief

He will wipe every tear from their eyes. There will be no more death or mourning or crying or pain, for the old order of things has passed away. He who was seated on the throne said, "I am making everything new!"

*Revelation 21:4-5*

Gladness and joy will overtake them, and sorrow and sighing will flee away.

*Isaiah 35:10*

My comfort in my suffering is this: Your promise preserves my life.

*Psalm 119:50*

*Here's something you can't dream your way out of ... think your way out of, buy your way out of, or work your way out of ... This is something you can only trust your way out of.*

*Bob Buford*

Though He brings grief, He will show compassion, so great is His unfailing love.

*Lamantations 3:32*

The Lord is close to the brokenhearted and saves those who are crushed in spirit.

*Psalm 34:18*

He heals the brokenhearted and binds up their wounds.

*Psalm 147:3*

Blessed are those who mourn, for they will be comforted.

*Matthew 5:4*

*God, it has been said, does not comfort us to make us comfortable, but to make us comforters. Where nobody suffers, nobody cares.*

*W.T. Purkiser*

# Guidance

For this God is our God for ever and ever; He will be our guide even to the end.

*Psalm 48:14*

Trust in the Lord with all your heart and lean not on your own understanding; in all your ways acknowledge Him, and He will make your paths straight.

*Proverbs 3:5-6*

Your word is a lamp to my feet and a light for my path.

*Psalm 119:105*

*When we depend on organizations, we get what organizations can do; when we depend on education, we get what education can do; when we depend on man, we get what man can do; but when we depend on prayer, we get what God can do.*

*A.C. Dixon*

Whether you turn to the right or to the left, your ears will hear a voice behind you, saying, "This is the way; walk in it."

*Isaiah 30:21*

I will instruct you and teach you in the way you should go; I will counsel you and watch over you.

*Psalm 32:8*

Yet I am always with You; You hold me by my right hand. You guide me with Your counsel, and afterward You will take me into glory.

*Psalm 73:23-24*

*Cast yourself into the arms of God and be very sure that if He wants anything of you, He will fit you for the work and give you strength.*

*Philip Neri*

# Guidance

The Lord will guide you always ...

*Isaiah 58:11*

He guides me in paths of righteousness for His name's sake.

*Psalm 23:3*

When He, the Spirit of truth, comes, He will guide you into all truth ... He will tell you what is yet to come.

*John 16:13*

I will give you shepherds after My own heart, who will lead you with knowledge and understanding.

*Jeremiah 3:15*

*Look around you and be distressed, look within you and be depressed, look to Jesus and be at rest.*

*Unknown*

Anyone who hates his brother is a murderer, and you know that no murderer has eternal life in him.

*1 John 3:15*

Love your neighbor as yourself. If you keep on biting and devouring each other, watch out or you will be destroyed by each other.

*Galatians 5:14-15*

If anyone says, "I love God," yet hates his brother, he is a liar. For anyone who does not love his brother, whom he has seen, cannot love God, whom he has not seen.

*1 John 4:20*

*He that returns a good for evil obtains the victory.*
*Thomas Fuller*

# Hate

Anyone who claims to be in the light but hates his brother is still in the darkness. Whoever loves his brother lives in the light, and there is nothing in him to make him stumble.

*1 John 2:9-10*

If you love those who love you, what reward will you get? And if you greet only your brothers, what are you doing more than others?

*Matthew 5:46-47*

A malicious man disguises himself with his lips, but in his heart he harbors deceit. His malice may be concealed by deception, but his wickedness will be exposed in the assembly.

*Proverbs 26:24-26*

*Hate is a prolonged form of suicide.*

*Douglas V. Steere*

In my vision at night I looked, and there before me was One like a son of man, coming with the clouds of heaven. He approached the Ancient of Days and was led into His presence. He was given authority, glory and sovereign power; all peoples, nations and men of every language worshiped Him. His dominion is an everlasting dominion that will not pass away, and His kingdom is one that will never be destroyed.

*Daniel 7:13-14*

No eye has seen, no ear has heard, no mind has conceived what God has prepared for those who love Him ...

*1 Corinthians 2:9*

*Where imperfection ceaseth, heaven begins.*

*P.J. Bailey*

# Heaven

In My Father's house are many rooms ... I am going there to prepare a place for you. And if I go and prepare a place for you, I will come back and take you to be with Me that you also may be where I am.

*John 14:2-3*

To him who overcomes, I will give the right to sit with Me on My throne, just as I overcame and sat down with My Father on His throne.

*Revelation 3:21*

"I tell you the truth, no one can enter the kingdom of God unless he is born of water and the Spirit."

*John 3:5*

*The same hand that made trees and fields and flowers, the seas and hills, the clouds and sky, has been making a home for us called heaven.*

*Billy Graham*

Now we know that if the earthly tent we live in is destroyed, we have a building from God, an eternal house in heaven, not built by human hands.

*2 Corinthians 5:1*

Our citizenship is in heaven. And we eagerly await a Savior from there, the Lord Jesus Christ, who, by the power that enables Him to bring everything under His control, will transform our lowly bodies so that they will be like His glorious body.

*Philippians 3:20-21*

*Anyone can devise a plan by which good people may go to Heaven. Only God can devise a plan whereby sinners, who are His enemies, can go to Heaven.*

*Lewis Sperry Chafer*

## Holiness

He chose us in Him before the creation of the world to be holy and blameless in His sight.

*Ephesians 1:4*

Once you were alienated from God and were enemies in your minds because of your evil behavior. But now He has reconciled you by Christ's physical body through death to present you holy in His sight, without blemish and free from accusation ...

*Colossians 1:21-22*

Create in me a pure heart, O God, and renew a steadfast spirit within me.

*Psalm 51:10*

*The Bible teaches that you don't determine a persons' greatness by the value of their wealth but by the wealth of their values.*

*Rick Warren*

You are a chosen people, a royal priesthood, a holy nation, a people belonging to God, that you may declare the praises of Him who called you out of darkness into His wonderful light.

*1 Peter 2:9*

He has raised up a horn of salvation for us ... to enable us to serve Him without fear in holiness and righteousness before Him all our days.

*Luke 1:69, 74-75*

Make every effort to live in peace with all men and to be holy; without holiness no one will see the Lord.

*Hebrews 12:14*

*We ask ourselves: 'Who am I to be brilliant, gorgeous, talented and fabulous?'. Actually, who are you not to be? You are a child of God.*

*Nelson Mandela*

## Holiness

Let us purify ourselves from everything that contaminates body and spirit, perfecting holiness out of reverence for God.

*2 Corinthians 7:1*

God did not call us to be impure, but to live a holy life. Therefore, he who rejects this instruction does not reject man but God, who gives you His Holy Spirit.

*1 Thessalonians 4:7-8*

I am the Lord your God; consecrate yourselves and be holy, because I am holy.

*Leviticus 11:44*

*God does not ask for the dull, weak, sleepy acquiescence of indolence. He asks for something vivid and strong. He asks us to cooperate with Him, actively willing what He wills, our only aim, His glory.*

*Amy Carmichael*

May He strengthen your hearts so that you will be blameless and holy in the presence of our God and Father ...

*1 Thessalonians 3:13*

But you were washed, you were sanctified, you were justified in the name of the Lord Jesus Christ and by the Spirit of our God.

*1 Corinthians 6:11*

Just as He who called you is holy, so be holy in all you do; for it is written: "Be holy, because I am holy."

*1 Peter 1:15-16*

*As a good Christian should consider every place holy because God is there, so he should look upon every part of his life as a matter of holiness because it is to be offered unto God.*

*William A. Law*

# Hope

Those who hope in the Lord will renew their strength. They will soar on wings like eagles; they will run and not grow weary, they will walk and not be faint.

*Isaiah 40:31*

The eyes of the Lord are on those who fear Him, on those whose hope is in His unfailing love ...

*Psalm 33:18*

Through Him you believe in God, who raised Him from the dead and glorified Him, and so your faith and hope are in God.

*1 Peter 1:21*

*If the blind put their hand in God's they find their way more surely than those who see but have not faith or purpose.*

*Helen Keller*

Find rest, O my soul, in God alone; my hope comes from Him.

*Psalm 62:5*

May the God of hope fill you with all joy and peace as you trust in Him, so that you may overflow with hope by the power of the Holy Spirit.

*Romans 15:13*

For You have been my hope, O Sovereign Lord, my confidence since my youth. From birth I have relied on You ...

*Psalm 71:5-6*

Be strong and take heart, all you who hope in the Lord.

*Psalm 31:24*

*God can pick sense out of a confused prayer.*
*Richard Sibbes*

## Hope

In His great mercy He has given us new birth into a living hope through the resurrection of Jesus Christ from the dead ...

*1 Peter 1:3*

Let us hold unswervingly to the hope we profess, for He who promised is faithful.

*Hebrews 10:23*

Everything that was written in the past was written to teach us, so that through endurance and the encouragement of the Scriptures we might have hope.

*Romans 15:4*

*The hidden glory of salvation is that everyone gets a chance to start over in life.*

*Calvin Miller*

If My people, who are called by My name, will humble themselves and pray and seek My face and turn from their wicked ways, then I will hear from heaven and will forgive their sin and will heal their land.

*2 Chronicles 7:14*

Your beauty should be that of your inner self, the unfading beauty of a gentle and quiet spirit, which is of great worth in God's sight.

*1 Peter 3:3-4*

A man's pride brings him low, but a man of lowly spirit gains honor.

*Proverbs 29:23*

*Nobody is too good for the meanest service.*
*Dietrich Bonhoeffer*

# Humility

"Blessed are the meek, for they will inherit the earth."

*Matthew 5:5*

He guides the humble in what is right and teaches them His way.

*Psalm 25:9*

"Whoever exalts himself will be humbled, and whoever humbles himself will be exalted."

*Matthew 23:12*

The Lord sustains the humble but casts the wicked to the ground.

*Psalm 147:6*

*Solitude is one of the deepest disciplines of the spiritual life because it crucifies our need for importance and prominence.*

*Richard Foster*

Do you see a man wise in his own eyes? There is more hope for a fool than for him.

*Proverbs 26:12*

"If anyone wants to be first, he must be the very last, and the servant of all."

*Mark 9:35*

Humble yourselves, therefore, under God's mighty hand, that He may lift you up in due time.

*1 Peter 5:6*

The fear of the Lord teaches a man wisdom, and humility comes before honor.

*Proverbs 15:33*

*Live through me, Son of God, make me like Thy clear air through which unhindered colors pass as though it were not there.*

*Amy Carmichael*

# Humility

Let another praise you, and not your own mouth;
someone else, and not your own lips.

*Proverbs 27:2*

If someone strikes you on one cheek, turn to him
the other also ... Give to everyone who asks you,
and if anyone takes what belongs to you, do not
demand it back. Do to others as you would have
them do to you.

*Luke 6:29-31*

Do nothing out of selfish ambition or vain con-
ceit, but in humility consider others better than
yourselves.

*Philippians 2:3*

*We waste too many of our prayers praying for the
other person to change, when some really honest
prayer for ourselves may do wonders.*

*Bruce Larson*

He has showed you, O man, what is good. And what does the Lord require of you? To act justly and to love mercy and to walk humbly with your God.

*Micah 6:8*

Be completely humble and gentle; be patient, bearing with one another in love.

*Ephesians 4:2*

If anyone thinks he is something when he is nothing, he deceives himself.

*Galatians 6:3*

Let him who boasts, boast in the Lord.

*2 Corinthians 10:17*

*The Christian on his knees sees more than the philosopher on tiptoe.*

*D.L. Moody*

# Humility

The Lord takes delight in His people; He crowns the humble with salvation.

*Psalm 149:4*

Whoever humbles himself like this child is the greatest in the kingdom of heaven.

*Matthew 18:4*

The eyes of the arrogant man will be humbled and the pride of men brought low; the Lord alone will be exalted in that day.

*Isaiah 2:11*

Pride goes before destruction, a haughty spirit before a fall.

*Proverbs 16:18*

*Learn the lesson that, if you are to do the work of a prophet, what you need is not a scepter but a hoe.*
*Bernard of Clairvaux*

Rid yourselves of all malice and all deceit, hypocrisy, envy, and slander of every kind.

*1 Peter 2:1*

Keep your lives free from the love of money and be content with what you have ...

*Hebrews 13:5*

Do not let your heart envy sinners, but always be zealous for the fear of the Lord.

*Proverbs 23:17*

*Our broken lives are not lost or useless. God's love is still working. He comes in and takes the calamity and uses it victoriously, working out His wonderful plan of love.*

*Eric Liddell*

# Jealousy

Where you have envy and selfish ambition, there you find disorder and every evil practice.

*James 3:16*

A heart at peace gives life to the body, but envy rots the bones.

*Proverbs 14:30*

I saw that all labor and all achievement spring from man's envy of his neighbor. This too is meaningless ...

*Ecclesiastes 4:4*

*We will never be released from emotions such as hatred or jealousy until we realize that other people are not responsible for our happiness.*

*Neil Eskelin*

*Joy*

You turned my wailing into dancing, you removed my sackcloth and clothed me with joy, that my heart may sing to You and not be silent. O Lord my God, I will give You thanks forever.

*Psalm 30:11-12*

For You make me glad by Your deeds, O Lord; I sing for joy at the works of Your hands.

*Psalm 92:4*

Rejoice in the Lord always. I will say it again: Rejoice!

*Philippians 4:4*

*Happiness is never in our power and pleasure is. I doubt whether anyone who has tasted joy would ever, if both were in his power, exchange it for all the pleasure in the world.*

*C.S. Lewis*

# Joy

Though you have not seen Him, you love Him; and even though you do not see Him now, you believe in Him and are filled with an inexpressible and glorious joy ...

*1 Peter 1:8*

I will rejoice in the Lord, I will be joyful in God my Savior.

*Habakkuk 3:18*

You will go out in joy and be led forth in peace; the mountains and hills will burst into song before you, and all the trees of the field will clap their hands.

*Isaiah 55:12*

*The gloom of the world is but a shadow; behind it, yet within our reach is joy. Take joy ...*

*Fra Giovanni*

Let the righteous rejoice in the Lord and take refuge in Him; let all the upright in heart praise Him!

*Psalm 64:10*

We also rejoice in God through our Lord Jesus Christ, through whom we have now received reconciliation.

*Romans 5:11*

Sing to God, sing praise to His Name ... and rejoice before Him.

*Psalm 68:4*

*Your unhappiness ... is due not to a want of something outside of you, but to a want of something inside you. You were made for perfect happiness. No wonder everything short of God disappoints you.*

*Fulton Sheen*

# Joy

The ransomed of the Lord will return. They will enter Zion with singing; everlasting joy will crown their heads. Gladness and joy will overtake them, and sorrow and sighing will flee away.

*Isaiah 51:11*

I have told you this so that My joy may be in you and that your joy may be complete.

*John 15:11*

I will see you again and you will rejoice, and no one will take away your joy.

*John 16:22*

*You can increase your happiness by simply adding to the number of times you perform an act of kindness.*

*Norman Vincent Peale*

If I go up to the heavens, You are there; if I make my bed in the depths, you are there ... if I settle on the far side of the sea, even there Your hand will guide me, Your right hand will hold me fast.

*Psalm 139:8-10*

Then you will call, and the Lord will answer; you will cry for help, and He will say: Here am I.

*Isaiah 58:9*

He is at my right hand, I will not be shaken.

*Acts 2:25*

"And surely I am with you always, to the very end of the age."

*Matthew 28:20*

*Prayer is exhaling the spirit of man and inhaling the Spirit of God.*

*Edwin Keith*

## Loneliness

I am with you and will watch over you wherever you go ...

*Genesis 28:15*

And I will ask the Father, and He will give you another Counselor to be with you forever – the Spirit of truth ... you know Him, for He lives with you and will be in you. I will not leave you as orphans ...

*John 14:16-18*

Surely the Lord is in this place, and I was not aware of it.

*Genesis 28:16*

*We shall never encounter God in the moment when that encounter takes place. It's always after that we can say, "So that strange situation, that impression, that unexplainable event was God."*

*Jacques Ellul*

Love the Lord your God with all your heart and with all your soul and with all your strength.

*Deuteronomy 6:5*

This is love for God: to obey His commands.

*1 John 5:3*

"Whoever has My commands and obeys them, he is the one who loves Me. He who loves Me will be loved by My Father, and I too will love him and show Myself to him. If anyone loves Me, he will obey My teaching. My Father will love him, and We will come to him and make Our home with him."

*John 14:21, 23*

*He loves us unconditionally with an everlasting love. All He asks of us is that we respond to Him with the free will that He has given to us.*

*Nancie Carmichael*

## Love for God

Grace to all who love our Lord Jesus Christ with an undying love.

*Ephesians 6:24*

"'Love the Lord your God with all your heart and with all your soul and with all your strength and with all your mind' and; 'Love your neighbor as yourself.'"

*Luke 10:27*

Everyone who believes that Jesus is the Christ is born of God, and everyone who loves the Father loves His Child as well.

*1 John 5:1*

*Worship is giving God the best that He has given you. Whenever you get a blessing from God, give it back to Him as a love gift.*

*Oswald Chambers*

## Love for others

This is how we know what love is: Jesus Christ laid down His life for us. And we ought to lay down our lives for our brothers.

*1 John 3:16*

Let us love one another, for love comes from God. Everyone who loves has been born of God and knows God.

*1 John 4:7*

This is how we know that we love the children of God: by loving God and carrying out His commands.

*1 John 5:2*

*Be the living expression of God's kindness; kindness in your face, kindness in your eyes, kindness in your smile.*

*Mother Teresa*

# Love for others

And so we know and rely on the love God has for us. God is love. Whoever lives in love lives in God, and God in him.

*1 John 4:16*

About brotherly love we do not need to write to you, for you yourselves have been taught by God to love each another.

*1 Thessalonians 4:9*

"For God so loved the world that He gave His one and only Son, that whoever believes in Him shall not perish but have eternal life."

*John 3:16*

*The church is her true self only when she exists for humanity.*

*Dietrich Bonhoeffer*

## Love of God

Let us not love with words or tongue but with actions and in truth.

*1 John 3:18*

I am convinced that neither death nor life, neither angels nor demons, neither the present nor the future, nor any powers, neither height nor depth, nor anything else in all creation, will be able to separate us from the love of God that is in Christ Jesus our Lord.

*Romans 8:38-39*

Above all, love each other deeply, because love covers over a multitude of sins.

*1 Peter 4:8*

*To believers, Jesus says, 'Go!' But to the lost world, Jesus says, 'Come!'*

*Rick Warren*

# Love of God

Love is patient, love is kind. It does not envy, it does not boast, it is not proud. It is not rude, it is not self-seeking, it is not easily angered, it keeps no record of wrongs. Love does not delight in evil but rejoices with the truth. It always protects, always trusts, always hopes, always perseveres. Love never fails.

*1 Corinthians 13:4-8*

May your unfailing love rest upon us, O Lord, even as we put our hope in You.

*Psalm 33:22*

"I have loved you with an everlasting love; I have drawn you with loving-kindness."

*Jeremiah 31:3*

*Jesus Christ is middle C on the Christian keyboard of life.*

*Claude H. Rhea*

# Love of God

"A new command I give you: Love one another. As I have loved you, so you must love one another. By this all men will know that you are My disciples, if you love one another."

*John 13:34-35*

This is love: not that we loved God, but that He loved us and sent His Son as an atoning sacrifice for our sins.

*1 John 4:10*

This is my prayer: that your love may abound more and more in knowledge and depth of insight ...

*Philippians 1:9*

*Several times along my life's journey, I had nowhere to turn except into my heavenly Father's arms. There I remained quiet, soaking up His love for as long as I needed.*

*Jean Otto*

# Love of God

"Though the mountains be shaken and the hills be removed, yet My unfailing love for you will not be shaken nor My covenant of peace be removed," says the Lord, who has compassion on you.

*Isaiah 54:10*

The Lord is gracious and compassionate, slow to anger and rich in love.

*Psalm 145:8*

Because of His great love for us, God, who is rich in mercy, made us alive with Christ ...

*Ephesians 2:4-5*

We love because He first loved us.

*1 John 4:19*

*God's fingers can touch nothing but to mold it into loveliness.*

*George MacDonald*

Blessed are all who fear the Lord, who walk in His ways. You will eat the fruit of your labor; blessings and prosperity will be yours.

*Psalm 128:1-2*

He who ignores discipline despises himself, but whoever heeds correction gains understanding.

*Proverbs 15:32*

As obedient children, do not conform to the evil desires you had when you lived in ignorance.

*1 Peter 1:14*

Submit yourselves, then, to God.

*James 4:7*

*The world goes forward because in the beginning one man or a few were true to the light they saw and by living by it enabled others to see.*

*Harold Gray*

## Obedience

Blessed is the man who fears the Lord, who finds great delight in His commands. His children will be mighty in the land; the generation of the upright will be blessed. Wealth and riches are in his house, and his righteousness endures forever.

*Psalm 112:1-3*


If you obey My commands, you will remain in My love, just as I have obeyed My Father's commands and remain in His love.

*John 15:10*


"Whoever does the will of My Father in heaven is my brother and sister and mother."

*Matthew 12:50*

*The disciplined person is the person who can do what needs to be done when it needs to be done.*
*Richard Foster*

## Obedience

We have all had human fathers who disciplined us and we respected them for it. How much more should we submit to the Father of our spirits and live!

*Hebrews 12:9*

This is how we know that we love the children of God: by loving God and carrying out His commands. This is love for God: to obey His commands.

*1 John 5:2-3*

Everyone must submit himself to the governing authorities, for there is no authority except that which God has established.

*Romans 13:1*

*To be a witness ... means to live in such a way that one's life would not make sense if God did not exist.*
*Dorothy Day*

# Obedience

"Anyone who breaks one of the least of these commandments and teaches others to do the same will be called least in the kingdom of heaven, but whoever practices and teaches these commands will be called great in the kingdom of heaven."

*Matthew 5:19*

If they obey and serve Him, they will spend the rest of their days in prosperity and their years in contentment.

*Job 36:11*

*So often I simply react to a situation rather than remembering how my God would have me respond because of who He is and because of what He has said.*

*Kay Arthur*

Everyone who hears these words of Mine and puts them into practice is like a wise man who built his house on the rock. The rain came down, the streams rose, and the winds blew and beat against that house; yet it did not fall, because it had its foundation on the rock.

*Matthew 7:24-25*

Whatever you have learned or received or heard from me, or seen in me – put it into practice. And the God of peace will be with you.

*Philippians 4:9*

*When you believe in Christ, when you live with Him, love and good works just naturally flow. They come from living together with Christ; His good influence just rubs off on us.*

*Mark Ellingsen*

# Peace

Let the peace of Christ rule in your hearts, since as members of one body you were called to peace.

*Colossians 3:15*

Peacemakers who sow in peace raise a harvest of righteousness.

*James 3:18*

I will listen to what God the Lord will say; He promises peace to His people, His saints – but let them not return to folly.

*Psalm 85:8*

A heart at peace gives life to the body, but envy rots the bones.

*Proverbs 14:30*

*To clasp the hands in prayer is the beginning of an uprising against the disorder of the world.*

*Karl Barth*

Consider the blameless, observe the upright; there is a future for the man of peace.

*Psalm 37:37*

The Lord bless you and keep you; the Lord make His face shine upon you and be gracious to you; the Lord turn His face toward you and give you peace.

*Numbers 6:24-26*

The Lord gives strength to His people; the Lord blesses His people with peace.

*Psalm 29:11*

"Peace I leave with you; My peace I give you."
*John 14:27*

*If God doesn't seem to be giving you what you ask, maybe He's giving you something else.*
*Frederick Buechner*

# Peace

May the Lord of peace Himself give you peace at all times and in every way.

*2 Thessalonians 3:16*

For to us a child is born ... And He will be called Wonderful Counselor, Mighty God, Everlasting Father, Prince of Peace. Of the increase of His government and peace there will be no end.

*Isaiah 9:6-7*

I will grant peace in the land, and you will lie down and no one will make you afraid.

*Leviticus 26:6*

*The only complete cure for your bad nerves, as you call them, is to relax in the hands of God and know that He is now looking after your troubles, that He is now guiding you into the quiet waters of inner peace.*

*Norman Vincent Peale*

The peace of God, which transcends all understanding, will guard your hearts and your minds in Christ Jesus.

*Philippians 4:7*

Grace, mercy and peace from God the Father and from Jesus Christ, the Father's Son, will be with us in truth and love.

*2 John 1:3*

For He Himself is our peace ... He came and preached peace to you who were far away and peace to those who were near. For through Him we both have access to the Father by one Spirit.

*Ephesians 2:14, 17-18*

*Prayer is the peace of our spirit.*

*Jeremy Taylor*

## Perseverance

Blessed is the man who perseveres under trial, because when he has stood the test, he will receive the crown of life that God has promised to those who love Him.

*James 1:12*

But one thing I do: Forgetting what is behind and straining toward what is ahead, I press on toward the goal to win the prize for which God has called me heavenward in Christ Jesus.

*Philippians 3:13-14*

Let nothing move you. Always give yourselves fully to the work of the Lord, because you know that your labor in the Lord is not in vain.

*1 Corinthians 15:58*

*He who has a why to live, can bear with almost any how.*

*Victor Frankl*

Be strong and take heart and wait for the Lord.

*Psalm 27:14*

We have come to share in Christ if we hold firmly till the end the confidence we had at first.

*Hebrews 3:14*

We also rejoice in our sufferings, because we know that suffering produces perseverance; perseverance, character; and character, hope. And hope does not disappoint us, because God has poured out His love into our hearts by the Holy Spirit, whom He has given us.

*Romans 5:3-5*

*The most difficult prayer, and the prayer which, therefore, costs us the most striving, is persevering prayer, the prayer which faints not, but continues steadfastly until the answer comes.*

*O. Hallesby*

# Praise and worship

Praise the Lord with the harp; make music to Him on the ten-stringed lyre. Sing to Him a new song; play skillfully, and shout for joy.

*Psalm 33:2*

"A time is coming and has now come when true worshipers will worship the Father in spirit and truth, for they are the kind of worshipers the Father seeks. God is Spirit, and His worshipers must worship in spirit and in truth."

*John 4:23-24*

Is anyone happy? Let him sing songs of praise.

*James 5:13*

*Religion is adoration. The most fundamental need, duty, honor, and happiness of men is not petition or even contrition, nor again, even thanksgiving ... but adoration.*

*Friedrich von Hügel*

# Praise and worship

I will praise You with the harp for Your faithfulness, O my God; I will sing praise to You with the lyre, O Holy One of Israel. My lips will shout for joy when I sing praise to You – I, whom You have redeemed. My tongue will tell of Your righteous acts all day long ...

*Psalm 71:22-24*

All the nations You have made will come and worship before You, O Lord; they will bring glory to Your name.

*Psalm 86:9*

*A God you can fully understand would be less than yourself.*

*Flannery O'Connor*

## Praise and worship

Give thanks to the Lord, call on His name; make known among the nations what He has done. Sing to Him, sing praise to Him; tell of all His wonderful acts. Glory in His holy name; let the hearts of those who seek the Lord rejoice.

*1 Chronicles 16:8-10*

Let the word of Christ dwell in you richly as you teach and admonish one another with all wisdom, and as you sing psalms, hymns and spiritual songs with gratitude in your hearts to God.

*Colossians 3:16*

*To worship God is to ascribe the proper worth to God, to address God as He is worthy ... He is worthy of all the worth and honor we can give Him and then infinitely more.*

*Donald S. Whitney*

# Praise and worship

Great is the Lord and most worthy of praise; He is to be feared above all gods. Praise be to the Lord, the God of Israel, from everlasting to everlasting.

*1 Chronicles 16:25, 36*

Praise the Lord, O my soul. O Lord my God, You are very great; You are clothed with splendor and majesty. I will sing to the Lord all my life; I will sing praise to my God as long as I live.

*Psalm 104:1, 33*

*God is the owner; I'm the manager. Every resource, every blessing I have today is a gift of God.*
*John C. Maxwell*

## Praise and worship

If anyone serves, he should do it with the strength God provides, so that in all things God may be praised through Jesus Christ. To Him be the glory and the power for ever and ever.

*1 Peter 4:11*

I will praise You, O Lord, with all my heart; I will tell of all Your wonders. I will be glad and rejoice in You; I will sing praise to Your name, O Most High.

*Psalm 9:1-2*

Sing the glory of His name; make His praise glorious!

*Psalm 66:2*

*Worship is transcendent wonder.*

*Thomas Carlyle*

# Praise and worship

Praise be to the God and Father of our Lord Jesus Christ, who has blessed us in the heavenly realms with every spiritual blessing in Christ.

*Ephesians 1:3*

The Lord is my strength and my song; He has become my salvation. He is my God, and I will praise Him, my father's God, and I will exalt Him.

*Exodus 15:2*

For God is the King of all the earth; sing to Him a psalm of praise.

*Psalm 47:7*

*Worship is just a dignified, polite but very personal way of getting in touch with God.*

*Norman Richardson*

# Prayer

The eyes of the Lord are on the righteous and His ears are attentive to their cry ...

*Psalm 34:15*

"Therefore I tell you, whatever you ask for in prayer, believe that you have received it, and it will be yours."

*Mark 11:24*

"And when you pray, do not be like the hypocrites, for they love to pray standing in the synagogues and on the street corners to be seen by men ... But when you pray, go into your room, close your door and pray to your Father, who is unseen."

*Matthew 6:5-6*

*A man prayed, and at first he thought that prayer was talking. But he became more and more quiet until in the end he realized that prayer is listening.*

*Søren Kierkegaard*

"This, then, is how you should pray: Our Father in heaven, hallowed be Your name, Your kingdom come, Your will be done on earth as it is in heaven. Give us today our daily bread. Forgive us our debts, as we also have forgiven our debtors. And lead us not into temptation, but deliver us from the evil one."

*Matthew 6:9-13*

Confess your sins to each other and pray for each other so that you may be healed. The prayer of a righteous man is powerful and effective.

*James 5:16*

How gracious He will be when you cry for help! As soon as He hears, He will answer you.

*Isaiah 30:19*

*That is true prayer: being all ear for God.*
*Henri Nouwen*

# Prayer

Call to Me and I will answer you and tell you great and unsearchable things you do not know.

*Jeremiah 33:3*

This is the confidence we have in approaching God: that if we ask anything according to His will, He hears us.

*1 John 5:14*

We do not know what we ought to pray for, but the Spirit Himself intercedes for us with groans that words cannot express.

*Romans 8:26*

*No one can believe how powerful prayer is and what it can effect, except those who have learned it by experience.*

*Martin Luther*

I urge, then, first of all, that requests, prayers, intercession and thanksgiving be made for everyone – for kings and all those in authority ...

*1 Timothy 2:1-2*

Pray in the Spirit on all occasions with all kinds of prayers and requests ... be alert and always keep on praying for all the saints.

*Ephesians 6:18*

"Ask and it will be given to you; seek and you will find; knock and the door will be opened to you. For everyone who asks receives; he who seeks finds; and to him who knocks, the door will be opened."

*Matthew 7:7-8*

*Eastern meditation is an attempt to empty the mind;*
*Christian meditation is an attempt to fill the mind.*
*Richard Foster*

# Protection

I Myself will tend My sheep and have them lie down, declares the Sovereign Lord. I will search for the lost and bring back the strays. I will bind up the injured and strengthen the weak, but the sleek and the strong I will destroy. I will shepherd the flock with justice.

*Ezekiel 34:15-16*

The Lord will keep you from all harm – He will watch over your life; the Lord will watch over your coming and going both now and forevermore.

*Psalm 121:7-8*

*This is a wise, sane Christian faith: that a man commit himself, his life and his hopes to God; that God undertakes the special protection of that man; that therefore that man ought not to be afraid of anything!*

*George MacDonald*

When you pass through the waters, I will be with you; and when you pass through the rivers, they will not sweep over you. When you walk through the fire, you will not be burned; the flames will not set you ablaze. For I am the Lord, your God ...

*Isaiah 43:2-3*

I will lie down and sleep in peace, for You alone, O Lord, make me dwell in safety.

*Psalm 4:8*

But you are a shield around me, O Lord; you bestow glory on me and lift up my head.

*Psalm 3:3*

*A man with God on his side is always in the majority.*

*John Knox*

# Protection

Those who trust in the Lord are like Mount Zion, which cannot be shaken but endures forever. As the mountains surround Jerusalem, so the Lord surrounds His people ...

*Psalm 125:1-2*

Let all who take refuge in You be glad ... Spread Your protection over them, that those who love Your name may rejoice in You.

*Psalm 5:11*

*What is there then than can blight our Christian hope; for apparently there is no person, place or thing that can neutralize the exhilarating truth that God is never far from any of us.*

*James Turro*

If you confess with your mouth, "Jesus is Lord," and believe in your heart that God raised him from the dead, you will be saved.

*Romans 10:9*

Repent and be baptized in the name of Jesus Christ for the forgiveness of your sins.

*Acts 2:38*

"I am the way and the truth and the life. No one comes to the Father except through Me."

*John 14:6*

"I stand at the door and knock. If anyone hears My voice and opens the door, I will come in and eat with him, and he with Me."

*Revelation 3:20*

*God has His own secret stairway into every heart.*

*Anonymous*

# Salvation

Christ was sacrificed once to take away the sins of many people; and He will appear a second time, not to bear sin, but to bring salvation to those who are waiting for Him.

*Hebrews 9:28*

"Where two or three come together in My name, there am I with them."

*Matthew 18:20*

In repentance and rest is your salvation, in quietness and trust is your strength ... The Lord longs to be gracious to you; He rises to show you compassion.

*Isaiah 30:15, 18*

*Oh, how great peace and quietness would he possess who should cut off all vain anxiety and place all his confidence in God.*

*Thomas à Kempis*

Each of you should look not only to your own interests, but also to the interests of others.

*Philippians 2:4*

Nobody should seek his own good, but the good of others.

*1 Corinthians 10:24*

When you ask, you do not receive, because you ask with wrong motives, that you may spend what you get on your pleasures.

*James 4:3*

*The very heart and root of sin is an independent spirit. We erect the idol self, and not only wish others to worship, but worship it ourselves.*

*Richard Cecil*

## Strength

The Sovereign Lord is my strength; He makes my feet like the feet of a deer, He enables me to go on the heights.

*Habakkuk 3:19*

God is our refuge and strength, an ever-present help in trouble.

*Psalm 46:1*

Be strong in the Lord and in His mighty power.

*Ephesians 6:10*

I can do everything through Him who gives me strength.

*Philippians 4:13*

*God designed the human machine to run on Himself.*

*C.S. Lewis*

The eyes of the Lord range throughout the earth to strengthen those whose hearts are fully committed to Him.

*2 Chronicles 16:9*

The Lord is faithful and He will strengthen and protect you from the evil one.

*2 Thessalonians 3:3*

The Lord is my strength and my shield; my heart trusts in Him ...

*Psalm 28:7*

*Sometimes we feel that evil is winning. Then Easter comes to remind us that there is no grave deep enough, no seal imposing enough, no stone heavy enough, no evil strong enough to keep Christ in the grave.*

*James W. Moore*

## Strength

It is God who arms me with strength and makes my way perfect. He makes my feet like the feet of a deer; He enables me to stand on the heights.

*2 Samuel 22:33-34*

The Lord is my strength and my song; He has become my salvation. He is my God and I will praise Him ...

*Exodus 15:2*

For the foolishness of God is wiser than man's wisdom, and the weakness of God is stronger than man's strength.

*1 Corinthians 1:25*

*A mighty fortress is our God,*
*a bulwark never failing.*

*Martin Luther*

He will respond to the prayer of the destitute; He will not despise their plea.

*Psalm 102:17*

My flesh and my heart may fail, but God is the stength of my heart and my portion forever.

*Psalm 73:26*

Those who sow in tears will reap with songs of joy. He who goes out weeping, carrying seeds to sow, will return with songs of joy, carrying sheaves with him.

*Psalm 126:5-6*

*Health is a good thing, but sickness is far better, if it leads us to God.*

*J.C. Ryle*

# Temptation

Be self-controlled and alert. Your enemy the devil prowls around like a roaring lion looking for someone to devour. Resist him, standing firm in the faith ...

*1 Peter 5:8-9*

Because He Himself suffered when He was tempted, He is able to help those who are being tempted.

*Hebrews 2:18*

God is faithful; He will not let you be tempted beyond what you can bear. But when you are tempted, He will also provide a way so that you can stand up under it.

*1 Corinthians 10:13*

*Peace is not found by escaping temptations, but by being tried by them.*

*Thomas à Kempis*

If someone is caught in a sin, you ... should restore him gently. But watch yourself, or you also may be tempted.

*Galatians 6:1*

We do not have a high priest who is unable to sympathize with our weaknesses, but we have One who has been tempted in every way, just as we are – yet was without sin.

*Hebrews 4:15*

Consider it pure joy, my brothers, whenever you face trials of many kinds, because you know that the testing of your faith develops perseverance.

*James 1:2-3*

*Temptations are never so dangerous as when they come to us in a religious garb.*

*D.L. Moody*

# Thanksgiving

Through Jesus, therefore, let us continually offer to God a sacrifice of praise – the fruit of lips that confess His name.

*Hebrews 13:15*

We pray this in order that you may live a life worthy of the Lord and may please Him in every way: ... joyfully giving thanks to the Father, who has qualified you to share in the inheritance of the saints in the kingdom of light.

*Colossians 1:10-12*

Let us come before Him with thanksgiving and extol Him with music and song.

*Psalm 95:2*

*It ought to be as habitual to us to thank as to ask.*
*Charles Spurgeon*

# Thanksgiving

Give thanks in all circumstances, for this is God's will for you in Christ Jesus.

*1 Thessalonians 5:18*

Therefore, since we are receiving a kingdom that cannot be shaken, let us be thankful, and so worship God acceptably with reverence and awe ...

*Hebrews 12:28*

Let them give thanks to the Lord for His unfailing love and His wonderful deeds ...

*Psalm 107:8*

Give thanks to the Lord, for He is good; His love endures forever.

*Psalm 107:1*

*God has two dwellings: one in heaven, and the other in meek and thankful hearts.*

*Izaak Walton*

# Trust

Trust in the Lord with all your heart and lean not on your own understanding; in all your ways acknowledge Him, and He will make your paths straight.

*Proverbs 3:5-6*

Trust in the Lord and do good; dwell in the land and enjoy safe pasture. Delight yourself in the Lord and He will give you the desires of your heart.

*Psalm 37:3-4*

*God asks you and me to put our faith in Him and to believe that we can do whatever He asks us to do. He is mighty to uphold us and make us stand, He will support us and keep us from falling!*

*Joyce Meyer*

Offer right sacrifices and trust in the Lord.

*Psalm 4:5*

Anyone who trusts in Him will never be put to shame ... Everyone who calls on the name of the Lord will be saved.

*Romans 10:11, 13*

The Lord is good, a refuge in times of trouble. He cares for those who trust in Him ...

*Nahum 1:7*

Some trust in chariots and some in horses, but we trust in the name of the Lord our God.

*Psalm 20:7*

*Anxiety in human life is what squeaking and grinding are in machines that is not oiled. In life, trust is the oil.*

*Henry Ward Beecher*

# Trust

Let him who walks in the dark, who has no light, trust in the name of the Lord and rely on his God.

*Isaiah 50:10*

Command those who are rich in this present world not to be arrogant nor to put their hope in wealth, which is so uncertain, but to put their hope in God, who richly povides us with everything ...

*1 Timothy 6:17*

In You I trust, O my God. No one whose hope is in You will ever be put to shame, but they will be put to shame who are treacherous without excuse.

*Psalm 25:2-3*

*Prayer is our declaration of dependence.*
*David Jeremiah*

## Wisdom

If any of you lacks wisdom, he should ask God, who gives generously to all without finding fault, and it will be given to him. But when he asks, he must believe and not doubt ...

*James 1:5-6*

I will instruct you and teach you in the way you should go; I will counsel you and watch over you.

*Psalm 32:8*

I will praise the Lord, who counsels me; even at night my heart instructs me.

*Psalm 16:7*

*Who knows? God knows and what He knows is well and best. The darkness hideth not from Him, but glows clear as the morning or the evening rose of east or west.*

*C.G. Rossetti*

# Wisdom

The wisdom that comes from heaven is first of all pure; then peace-loving, considerate, submissive, full of mercy and good fruit, impartial and sincere.

*James 3:17*

He will be the sure foundation for your times, a rich store of salvation and wisdom and knowledge ...

*Isaiah 33:6*

Christ, in whom are hidden all the treasures of wisdom and knowledge.

*Colossians 2:2-3*

*We need some well of wisdom from which we can draw that will help us to get life back into focus ... We can gain the wisdom we need from Christ.*

*James E. Carter*

"For I will give you words and wisdom that none of your adversaries will be able to resist or contradict."

*Luke 21:15*

I keep asking that the God of our Lord Jesus Christ, the glorious Father, may give you the spirit of wisdom and revelation, so that you may know Him better.

*Ephesians 1:17*

For the Lord gives wisdom, and from His mouth comes knowledge ...

*Proverbs 2:6*

*All my discoveries have been made in answer to prayer.*

*Isaac Newton*

# Worry

Do not be anxious about anything, but in every-thing, by prayer and petition, with thanksgiving, present your requests to God. And the peace of God, which transcends all understanding, will guard your hearts and your minds in Christ Jesus.

*Phillippians 4:6-7*

An anxious heart weighs a man down, but a kind word cheers him up.

*Proverbs 12:25*

We wait in hope for the Lord; He is our help and our shield.

*Psalm 33:20*

*I am so absolutely certain that coming to know Him as He really is will bring unfailing comfort and peace to every troubled heart ...*

*H.W. Smith*

# Worry

Do not let your hearts be troubled. Trust in God, trust also in Me.

*John 14:1*

Cast all your anxiety on Him because He cares for you.

*1 Peter 5:7*

Do not worry about your life, what you will eat or drink; or about your body, what you will wear ... Look at the birds of the air; they do not sow or reap or store away in barns, and yet your heavenly Father feeds them. Are you not much more valuable than they? Who of you by worrying can add a single hour to his life? So do not worry ...

*Matthew 6:25-27, 31*

*God commands you to pray but forbids you to worry.*

*St. John Vianney*

## Worry

Tyranny will be far from you; you will have nothing to fear. Terror will be far removed; it will not come near you.

*Isaiah 54:14*

My soul finds rest in God alone; my salvation comes from Him.

*Psalm 62:1*

Do not fret because of evil men or be envious of those who do wrong ... Commit your way to the Lord; trust in Him ...

*Psalm 37:1, 5*

*No difficulties in your case can baffle Him ... If you will only put yourselves absolutely into His hands and let Him have His own way with you.*

*H.W. Smith*